MONDEGREEN RIFFS

Library and Archives Canada cataloguing in publication is available
upon request.

ISBN 978-1-998779-46-8

Printed and bound in Canada.

This book is printed on acid free paper that is 100% recycled ancient
forest friendly (100% post-consumer recycled).

First Edition

10 9 8 7 6 5 4 3 2 1

atbaypress.com

We acknowledge the support of the
Canada Council for the Arts.

With the generous support of the
Manitoba Arts Council.

MONDEGREEN
RIFFS

I Mishear the Most
Beautiful Things

**Angeline
Schellenberg**

Winnipeg

Lord, help me find it in my heart
to forgive you
for making me the way I am.
Blasphemy? Perhaps…

—Michael Moynahan, SJ

For Mary

A Bruised Reed

Triangle

bee

me

sea

see /

me   me   me   me   me   \

be

see bee   see thee   see me   see thee

see thee see me

thee me sea bee tree

\ we /

Magenta

Majestic form of gentle, cousin to all satisfied sighs—
aqua, wisteria. The only colour not found when white
light breaks into waves. Like soul mates, magenta
exists only in the mind. Midway between teen blush
and bruised plum, magenta is a marriage of equals. The
psychedelic point where rainbows overlap. Invented
by a teenager who, in mixing up a cure for malaria,
discovered mauve instead. Christened for the fuchsia
flower. Matisse's nipples and cold brown dwarf stars
appear magenta to the naked human eye. Possessed
by nonconformist brides and flamingos, my college
dormmate sang out *magen-TAAAH! Magen-TAAAH!* at
midnight, and you had to be there. Stare at magenta
long enough, and even the blank page grows green.

**Do potatoes have souls? Is there some sort
of experiment I could do to find out before
I mash them?**

How to speak of owning
the ethereal?

When the world was reborn,
we grew in the dark.
All eyes and hearts.

We are by nature tangential.
Rimmed in skin, reaching.

How did we learn,
from deep inside the earth,
the nature of light?

Xylophone

Play me the alphabet, dear zebu.
Vault on chopsticks through the yak bodega.

Just kick it up on the boardwalk, honeybee:
ice cream, eyelash, licorice whip.

Smart baby toes tap mama's ribs
and gut and navel.

Montezuma Oropendolas,
feather us a zephyr—quid pro quo.

Reflexes: check.

Chick, chalk,
cheek.

Chartreuse

An inchworm along the path from green to yellow, chartreuse unearths all we've lost (youth). Sprite's imaginary tint. The elixir of life—goes down easy as burgundy. Tender and electric, the grass roots I chewed at recess, the bottom of Clear Lake at 10 am. The heart of an avocado, the flesh of the pistachio, the soul of expression. Brings any tired room out of the box. Look: a fire engine visible in the darkness, fireweed bursting under the snuffed forest candles. Chartreuse puts the zing in aurora. Coats our old farmhouse in glam. The unripe pear skin, the lovebird's belly. It's the VW van we could push-start to Mexico, a bed of Scotch moss where you could lay me down.

Oboe

Flowery,
who me?

Sadness is innocence
keening.

I bite my lover's lower lip.
River's edge turns to ballad.

A marionette ballet.

Fill the hills with goats.

Flit.
Flourish.
Light-footed lamentation.

Taste this raspberry—
I insist.

Violet

Introvert hiding at the height of the visible. Geriatric and juvenile, pleats and thank-you. Hallow us with a gentle edge. Scribed in Japanese as *purity, lovely; lucidity, sound of jewels*. Oh vanity, vanity, stain bacteria into view. Mallow glow in Monet's ponds, the Arctic sunset. Sappho's bloom. Your eyes promising longevity. Viola of purple's ensemble. *Voila!* of spring.

Flute

filigree zephyr, scintillate sequin strings
in high spirits, sprites aspire

aspirate *ethereal*
apple blossom petals
on a wet, white bough

glittering champagne
new-year sigh, wafting lace

come nymph, Isis whispers

teasel's sessility cups sound
like water

suscipe
chickadees in the hereafter

Are skeletons real or made up?

What do we know
of what we hold inside,

of what holds us?

Cadavers are to humans
as silk is to sea.

Like butterflies
in a windowless aviary,

best to let the body
know what it knows

and never tells.

Silver

Everything we've never been handed on a platter: a shiver of mercury, sliver of moon. Sterling and refined, silver skates around lampposts. Snips loose ends. Jean Valjean read by candlelight, *Johnny Tremain* by the crack under the door. The spoon I was born into. A marriage that lasts until the children leave home. The handle on your coffin. A near-win. The lining we've been looking for. Lustrous. The ebb and flow of time. A vessel in the house of God. A stirring under the frozen lake of my pelvis.

Clarinet

Of black magic, of archipelago.

Dark chocolate slides
down the throat,
turns into moan.

Chrome. The alley narrows.

Wet hair glistening,
the woman on the screen descends
the stairs of her chateau.

Mistletoe. McConaughey's hand
along her chin. Tableau.

A calico to caress a calf.
Rise in moonlit dance, a willow.

In women are the lungs located in the breasts?

It is only loneliness.
This hive. This hill
that divides.

My chest, a cavity.
It is only loneliness,
this thing I swallowed.

The parachute rising
as I fall, breathless:
only loneliness.

Russet

Think subdued ruffle. Think settling hooves on cobblestone. Coarse homespun woe enervates Shakespearian regret—steadfast and sour in equal measure. Ruddiness of spud, rough apple skin brushed and paired with *barley harvest, swans mill cream,* or *dash of pepper.* Auburn hair and autumn sleeves. Fired clay, sparrow. There are no landmarks. Bend back the branch and clasp the cabin door behind you.

Bassoon

Boozy cocoa. Tapestry's
aroma. A monk lifts his glass.

A hairy-nosed wombat wobbles
toward extinction. The barefoot clown

walks home from the party, one shoe
under his arm. A muffler

rumbles through *la noche oscura*. Bundle of logs
by the fire.

We are touring
tunnels of prohibition, sections

of grapefruit in our teeth.

In a suit jacket, at a teak table, a demon
lays down his fork.

Is it okay to boil headphones?
Can I boil them to drive the evil out?

Water can only go so far.

Boil pasta. Watch as the water becomes noodly, but noodles stay noodle.

The best we can do is soften evil slightly. Make it vibrate to *goodness is good*.

Plastic—from *plastikos*—meaning *able to be shaped*.

Dip your ears under the lake and listen:

music in the unfurling light.

Not Love,
I Have Become Sounding Brass

Timpani

Oceanic.
Exhume cave song.

Insomnia,
a sonic < > < > < >!

Sing the bucket list
of sharks: try reindeer meat,
swim with caged humans.

Oh, rising sun!
This is the day I walk out
on my inhibitions.

Elbow room!
The here and now, a fulcrum.

On the one hand, an explosion.
On the other, an olive branch.

Scarlet

No one holds a candlestick to scarlet: stain of the heart, the embers, the tongue. More radiant than rage. Forbidden fruit. The sky before the storm. It drips from the nails of Christ. Rides the coattails of Mounties and the tailfins of Daddy's Chev. The town is painted, our hands are caught. Enflamed with lust or shame, everything depends upon the red we borrow. For centuries Europeans searched for the perfect red bugs to crush: *Kermes vermilio* scratched from the crotches of bur oak. Life preserver or siren's kiss? While crimson leans toward purple, scarlet rises like the cardinal, a hero in spandex. Scarlet is my inner fist. The fox no one hears.

Do the interiors of buildings cease to exist when people leave them?

How do our umbrella trees
return to us so effortlessly
as we re-enter?

How do our dictionaries
and chairs
find their places?

Do they mourn for us
or for themselves
when we go?

How do the lamps
sense our departure?
How long have we held
such power?

How do victims
disappear with a remote
click, a diminishing glow?

Why does grief
still spark inside my lids
whenever I close my eyes?

Trumpet

Brash bad boy
bringing a gander into battle.

If my point's a Camaro,
he'll drive it home.

Tight-lipped, slip ships
into Signal Hill.

Shrill. Brand the dizzy cattle
with bravado.

Dang it all. Don't give a damn
where the spit may fall.

Purple

Oh pomp and belly dance, oh soda fountain majesty, lift us to lofty places, call for prose! The ambiguity betwixt seeing red and feeling blue, stability electrified—stay post-partisan, leave our baggage at the store. Breathlessness of skin and nails, say *divine* or *retribution,* robe us in Lent or luxury. Evoke brooding or playful thoughts in the bedroom—and when I am old, I shall *purrrr.* We've forgotten: before chlorophyll, purple emblazoned every leaf. Purplery—pre-greenery, pre-dino. *With a great big hug and a kiss from me to you, won't you*…promise me a love I'm not so sure I wanted.

Trombone

Marble maze,
hello? Pick up the phone!
Clown around New Orleans,
you fizzy licorice twist, you,
hook us on your fool's errand.
Wanton faucet, yawn.
Let your stocking slip,
one-legged show girl,
let's blow this joint,
and give ol' boredom
the boot.
Golden garden hose,
grow and spawn!
Windshield-wipe the sky,
bellow odes to longhorn sheep
and plumbers.
Heroic flamingo, oh,
slide from your throne,
hoist your loopy trunk and blow:
metamorphose us
in your mellow meows.

How do you dress to look like a poet?

Lose your shoe. Artfully.
Like Bishop, *practice
losing faster.*

In your best sweats,
worry a hole
with your pen.

Wait
for the spiders
to mend them.

Find earrings
in the cirrus clouds.
Don't try to wear them.

Listen for robins,
but mimic the crow,
that ostentatious smile.

Dress for failure.
Now make your failures
glorious.

Euphonium

Soft pedal your unicycle through tall grass
bakeries, patrons humming and hawing
over fishbowls of yeasty fog.
A damp cloth on a feverish
foreboding takes the edge off.
Pussyfoot around cloudy issues
in your boathouse bootlaces,
peony blossom in your bosom.
Amid rare bookshop spines and pages
soft as syrup, a sweltering Bogart
hands you his final smoke.

Ochre

Whether you want to get decadent or down and dirty, ochre delivers. On the rusted edges of memory, the colour as old as the hills takes no bull. The effect of heat on dough, the kiss of ultraviolet on my skin. Spilling warm and rich, leaves a ring around chance meetings. Stimulate appetite in the kitchen, lust under a crinkling foil. From the nose of the obsequious to the lunch bag of the frugal: the colour of a religious habit. The topsoil of first impressions. The optimism of my fading bruise. Rarely declared the favourite, ochre is the first crayon to disappear into the woodwork; it sinks into the ground, buries itself in fur, camouflages everything wild that's escaping.

Do you think humans will ever walk on the sun?

Some night when solar storms
throw off their feathers,

we'll ascend through waxen clouds
and all their serenades.

Hang on a little longer, my dear.
This season may be dark but it's only

the sort of darkness
you'd find under the shadow

of a wing.

French Horn

Cathedral winds haunting, labyrinthine.
A huntsman holds up the tender moon
and snails spiral open. Ah, how the skirts
of languid films spin galaxies into being, planets
whorling velvet waves. Suave middle child amid
holiday hoo-ha, pour out your cornucopia.
Warm vanilla in smears of cream. Sustain us.
Sonorous, the rams mourn.
Their breath levitates above the pines.
A messiah lets down his shroud.
A balm, abide.
Selah.

Beige

A good beige whispers of violets or caramel. Less kinky than khaki, more sunlit than drab, beige is the builder of neutral ground between minivans. Though it's buff and tan, beige is never dated; it's the nine-to-fiver who doesn't stray from path or pack. Sleepy music of sand, brush of fawn and mushroom, the best thing since buttered toast. In tones from diminuendo to the silence after the final chord. Warm as bisque, solid as a tusk. When an astronaut walked into a Starbucks, the average colour of the universe was christened *Cosmic latte*. With paint names like *accessible, balanced,* and *barley,* it may be a drop cloth for your anxious musings. Publicly maligned, privately hoarded, like ballet flats and gratitude, it goes with anything. Even Matisse's *Joy of Life* fades to beige—a chemical reaction to light. French for freshly shorn wool, it reveals what others are hiding: texture, angle, depth. Beige pushes wallflowers onto dance floors. Makes a red lampshade sing. Comfy as dumplings and oatmeal, while they say you can be beiged to death, deep down you know it would be completely painless.

**Whenever I see the map of the world, "all"
the countries are on one side, how come they
never show the other side of the map?**

In space, no up or down.

Who's to say we've come out on top?
We split the atom but left a page unread.

There's so much our one-sided guides
will never show us.

What do you say we dismount
an expedition?

I have a desire
to leave this basement. I have a rope.

The world: fathoms-wide and oh so shallow.

Let's stop our digging
and go where gold lies on the surface.

To an unspoiled land
made just for those who take the leap.

Tuba

Rumble underwater
consolation.

Some days you got to go down
before you can get up again.

Holy Jupiter, dust off
those ostinato mushrooms.

Bison-headed, you're
no fuddy-duddy.

Rise and fall like a Goodyear.

A T-Rex laying eggs
on the long march to the Gobi.

The human womb echoes
land masses groaning.
Cavernous and grave.

I was bitten by a turtle when I was a young lad, can I still drink orange juice?

One Lego hand reached
inside a small boy's nose
and stayed. A working flash drive
was recovered from a leopard seal's frozen feces.
Skin talks. We cannot silence it.
Wedding rings grow on carrots.
Old fishers reel in the wallets
of childhood schoolmates. Parrots return,
speaking Spanish, singing the opening lines
of The Good, The Bad, and the Ugly.
Here's how it goes: a researcher
found a seal who had eaten
a sea bird who had eaten the flash drive
dropped by a kayaker.
Sometimes, it's just that unclouded.
I don't need to tell you,
two years later when the boy bent
over a plate of pink cupcakes
and inhaled, he felt a pain
and found his missing piece.

Indigo

Contraceptive, aphrodisiac, Levis. Bluest blue with power to bewitch, catch every hair, every fibre with a stain, indelible, transcending. Devil's dye. Camels crossed the Sahara carrying indigo, ivory, salt, and slaves. (A length of blue cotton could buy a life.) Incense to ward off evil. Colonizers sent white cloth to "civilize Africa." Nigerian women used stitch resist and paste resist and many trips to the indigo bath: erased colonizers' prints. Tattoo, tincture. Mayans mixed clay with indigo to create a blue that souls could carry to the underworld. Eye shadow, salve. A woman devoured the sky. God pulled the sky higher.

Before a Word Is on My Tongue

Gong

This is my Moment

> the Soon and
> the Not Yet of it

(((((guiltpang)))))

Once struck
Awe cannot be controlled ((((((((((((

Fall to your knees

Now
> and

How long can you keep a brain alive outside the body?

My first clarinet lesson, teacher's red flannel belly, white undershirt between the buttons. He presses my knuckles onto his gut. *Punch me. Hard.* My family doesn't hug. *Make your diaphragm this hard, so hard that if someone punches you*

it won't hurt. They say I have a voice to hide in a choir. In the choir loft they watch my body. Does anyone hear the words?

In the tape deck *Morning Like This* is jubilant! *Disgusting! The ground gets its thrills from feeling Christ's feet?* Sensation is sex is sick. *Say no.*

In the honour band I get first chair. I'll live alone. Strangers will love me.

Curve your fingers, raise the roof of your mouth,
tighten your embouchure.   Think think   think.
Feel feel   feel.   Never

love. When Dad feels stress his inner ear attacks.
Vertigo. I make my body weightless, footsteps silent.
Or wake the jet inside his skull.

The boy. If only he would hold me while I cry.
Wishing in bed is sex is sick. Say no. I try…

…to write but a falsetto line…*on the inside, on which*
side…The carnival ride

goes round and round. *Only on the cheek. Until he lifts*
the veil. Rock races your heart to the beat of the thrust.
Sensation is sex is. Cast party conga line, hands-on-hips
and sagging socks—no thoughts. Waiting for my ride:

I am going to hell.

Raise your hands! I peek across the pew at
worshippers in ecstasy. *Lift up your voice!* Leaving me
behind. Why are there no lips or lids for our ears?

Across the lake a sudden radio. Silence is broken. Tell
me I'm not

the only one who feels it rupture. At the symphony a
bass drum beats

my chest, the violinists scrape their bows across my
arms, my arms across my heart hold intact my ribs,
palms over my ears

to keep the violence out. Sensory. Sorry.

You're not feeling the music. Textbook says cheeks
should flush. When we kiss, I run to the girls' mirror to
check. I identify as heteroromantic, amusical.

I wish to hear less.

Instead, my brain transforms dying pitch to phantom
sound. Tinnitus: the scream only I can hear. Before Easter

trumpet blast I suspend my feet above thumping floor.
Rattles through my chair into my thighs. Even if I lose
all my hearing

no escape. I'm trying to make you hear

how it feels. I am alone.

At my first poetry reading my brain

becomes bee, becomes honey. Ahhh. This is what
other bodies

feel when they sing. When the music starts, my hands
fly

to my heart to sign the words. Meaning flows through
my fingers. On my page

I give music pronouns: *I, she, you*. Translate sound
into a someone I could love.

Azure

The blister pack around autumn. Watery stone, jewelled sea—every element but fire, always under and above us. My thoughts from far away. Halfway between sad and cyan, hovering over hyperlinks, milkweed. For Kandinsky, the sky awoke desire for the eternal; in Kuznetsov, the exotic. By its name, azure promises certainty. The purr of a tongue tracing the coastline of my ear.

Is it possible to make a new letter and put it in the alphabet?

At the beginning
of the phrase, it would have substance:

like a grape between your teeth, a stone
skipped across the lake at dusk.

It would lift off your lips
into the squirrel-shaped clouds.

Look up: dragonflies
are eating vowels above your head.

Your letter is a child carried up to bed.
She only pretends to be asleep.

Saxophone

sinew sizzle razor
debate and muscle

incarnate rare steak
alligator cane

sunset riffraff

pizzazz as far as you can s p i t
Lazarus does a double take

hazard a double-fried moxie

drinking cadmium
baptize a squirrel braying

caffeine hotline
tangerine shenanigan
crusty roll cactus

muzzle caterpillar
monkeyshines grease

edge of silence {weep}

Orange

Rhymer of nothing. Swirling the rec room of the spanking years. Truth segmented. Puts the carrot before the horse. Clearcuts the bookstores to build Amazon. Did I ever hold a Popsicle to the sun? If this book's cover is orange, I'll burn it. Goldfish, spray tans, redheads. In fifteenth-century Europe, orange existed without a name. Bee in my bonnet. Turmeric, tamarack: a different drum. If you bring orange inside my house, I'll eat you.

How to get YouTube to come film you? I have some funny things to show the internet. I have been calling, calling, and calling.

This whale of a disconnect,
so hard to breach.

The nuthatch sings in shutter clicks
with nothing to show for it.

If life is a ballgame,
can I be your empire?

Mourning dove,
more *woo* than *ta-da*.

Our heads like ducks, our dresses
without pockets, and our double sinks.

If life is a prison,
let me be your cufflinks.

The cat on my tongue,
too bagged to let out.

I don't think I talk to myself…
but maybe I'm just not listening.

If life is a circus,
will you be my ringtone?

Turquoise

Praise to the vintage fridge that hums my Granny's prayers. French for "Turkish": *le café* romanced by the bazaar. *I think I hear your mood ringing.* Beneath our feet: tiny tablets inscribed with the Creator's laugh lines. The only jade vine beguiles bats into a cascade of elf shoe blooms. Yes, Wordsworth, let's stoop, let others soar. Fallen sky, leak into the crevices that remain; soak up copper for blue, iron for green, form veins. Jewels clasp mother rock, revealing me: serene as spider silk, strong as robin's egg. Turn wise, tranquil eyes. As it was and will be.

Do cats have regional dialects?

Sense and common loons. Uncommon libraries.
Et tu brewing? Storms before eyes
except after nudes.

It's all two down, one étude in, see minor
flaws in the ointment—not what I
accept after noon. All knobs lead to roads.

Floss, I meant. A scent too dour
to calm a bruise. Storms elude
the land of the lie.

Cymbal

Razzmatazz.   (((((((( ))))))))

I'm here for you, birthday girl.   ((()))

Hit me with a Snakebite.

An anvil walks into a bar.

Stop me if you've heard this one.

Jet

A perfect backdrop to starry eyes and orphaned mornings. From the ambiguity of rubber boots to the persuasiveness of that little dress, jet travels well. It's the line between success and obscurity, a rebellious streak of pigment, the priesthood of all that's swanky, solvent, underground. Any depressed typewriter key, the raised flag of punk and piracy. Like the last licorice twist, it screams: I'm in control. It's the sheen of vinyl records as they spin, plunging velvet backs onto supple leather. Raven or phantom, the absence of light behind your eyes, an entire spectrum dancing on the head of a pin. Pitch: how the pot sounds to the whistling kettle. Black are the names of sheep who don't count, cats who've crossed over. Apocalyptic horse of hunger, the ever-ready battery of hi-tech discomforts, the big-box death that tramples thanksgiving. Symbol of grief, the black widow spider consumes what she cannot love.

Why are the holes in cats' fur always in the right place for their eyes?

the hairdresser sections off my hair
runs strands through her fingers

her warm iron lets go   *ah*
in a burst of steam
curls falling warm across my shoulders

no one can say
how one person finds another

a dandelion finds a rift
in the concrete

my hands find the clarinet keys
though I could not tell you
which finger will find   C
until it sounds

Aqua

À qui? Pourquoi? Soothing quandary of blue versus green versus oblivion. Cyan incubated. Mint submerged. Sea glass mason jars in a quaint cabana, pool bottom quavering. Smooth your soul. Soap up. Aqua Velva, after all, is afraid of nothing. Naughty, serene as Curaçao liqueur. Quaff. Uncap your *n'importe quoi. On y va?*

Bass Guitar

Zip fear, shroom.

Subtle bobbleheads overdub hubbub.
Dubious aboma.

Audible anathema,
bubinga.

Scrubby subshrub.
Backward pubescent sub-zero bubaline
flubdub.

Élan, aplomb. Intrepid bubble.

Publish subversive clubs.
Aftermath sublime
aswarm with subtitles.

Scratch that.
Troubled troubadour, succumb.

Gold

Ribbon around all that glitters: Globes, Fates. My retriever's ear. The tooth we couldn't heal. A bridge over despondency. Leaps of faith I'm glad I didn't take. (This poem cost me a fortune in therapy.) Thin layer of guilt. The grooved halos of *I do*. Silence is. God's thoughts buried since the dawn of time, imperishable as the rule we live by. Unto. Unto. Undone. Glorious are the gathered edges of my onion skin pages, the hairs tickling my legs. The years I have yet to feel.

Is having a dog a sign of communistic behaviour?

The animal is a sign of a need, surely—
one that we're too frightened
to say out loud.

Not a need to hold each other,
necessarily. Not the need of weak-willed men
to tell someone when to sit or fetch.

Perhaps it is a need to know
the scraps falling from our table
are not wasted,

or know the hairs
on our carpets are not our own.

Vladimir Lenin had a cat that he posed with
but never named.

Piano

Skunk in the trunk.
This seaboard is discord.

Run amuck,   a ghost aghast.

Anti-wrinkle hoodwinks.
Free think,   head shrink.   Glot. Glot.
Bespeckle inkblots.

Tell the truth through your teeth.   Wink, wink.
Fall on your face with grace.
I know what you did, honey.

The elephant in the closed set.
The skeleton's got the broom.

Hang ylang-ylang.   Pinstripe petunia.
Bon bon.   Bye bye, tsetse fly.

Tiptoe through the tiger paws; odds are fifty-fifty even
if you pinky swear.

Play chiropractic along my vertebrae. Cows roll.
Baby, toss me a doily
when you get the upper hand.

For mine are the keys,
the hammers,
the flurry.
Forever endeavour.
Amends.

Stretch out Your Hand

Celesta

Divinity: the stars that
fling hands into space.

Let's walk on seashells
around each other.

See, there's a change
in your shadow.

Wait…while I slip into
a more comfortable
orchid.

Ecru

Undertones are having a moment. Shadowed egret. Old French for *crude*. Pre-furred backstory: a leopard can assuage its thoughts. I feel unprepared. (But let me whip up a miracle.) Purity culture left untreated. Accrue interest in what comes naturally. Raw to the bone. I read our open palms. The flesh beneath my negligee— nubbly as unfinished silk.

Is the earth visible from earth? Just wondering...

Where Now and Always cross
like hoofmarks in the sand, lie down,

look up: the glowing belly of a gull.
Feel your stomach flip.

They say the unreflective sky
envies the lake.

If you stand on a mountain,
you may not see the summit.

If you hold a child to your breast,
you cannot see his face.

His fingers grasp your sleeve.
Pull the curtain back.

Viola

In the shadows
a pearl glows
a mourning dove
I spread my wings
and sing the still small
lung awake
though no one
knows my name

Chalk White

Settling dead plankton turning colourless acid turning *a hundred times after school*. The fog follows. A lab coat tells me to hold still. Fluorescents. Fans. White is the noise I *do* hear. My pillow sham's next-to-godliness. Pure as forgiven snow. Grit my teeth. The blank screen welcomes the ghost of an idea. Cough up the dust.

What is heavier: a kilogram of steel or a kilogram of feathers? I know they both weigh the same, but I don't know which is heavier.

The months since
I found her breathless
pass quickly.

The foil *Get Well*
balloons on the ceiling
floated for weeks
above her empty bed.

They say the fear
of death can give
a body enough strength
to lift a car.

This locket containing
her ashes
presses itself
into my palm,

my palm into the table,
the table into the earth.
The earth as it hurtles
toward heaven.

Pipe Organ

Ah   omniscient lung
Devotion's smokestack

Exhale the held
Breath of bridegrooms in their sharp
Black shoes

Ascend wassailing whale song
A responsive deity quakes dust down

Ezekiel's eyes on every side

Console   swell to great
Every extremity   strains

Ivory

The elephant in the room. Dreams of hand-me-down crochet that tower. Roll the dice. Citrus-scented nosegay. Pearls tumble. There is a beach found only in my dream. Exposed as my dog's belly. Cold cream melts down my father's wrist as I say, *I'm pregnant*. Waves of surrender: *he loves me, he loves me not*.

Are there birds in Canada?

I made our marriage therapist
miss them.

We were still on her sofa, I was still
on her sofa beside you, I was on
her sofa crying

when the Canadian Forces Snowbirds
flew over

in nine-part harmony, spinning
closer to one another
than we dare,

their beautiful, dangerous bodies—
arms outstretched.

Pink

Colour of the interior: salmon, watermelon. The living human brain before it fades to grey. Apple blossoms rain between my baby's toes. Pinkwash the bin of rakes in support of breasts. German orphanages dressed boys in pink, girls in blue like the Virgin Mother. Between the World Wars, the West confined pink, pregnant and barefoot, to kitsch. The icing on the cake. In my dreams, it predicts success. In your urine, cancer. Named for the jagged flower's prick. Safe as Barbie's sealed vulva. Pink stands with the kid pressed up against the chain-link. Slip of the tongue. My brothers' earplugs. The marks across their cheeks. I could not save us.

How am I sure I am the real mom of my kid?

I think *breathe*　my chest rises.
Hmm　and in my throat, a buzz.

This uterus— beyond me. A geode.
Break open this dull stone.

Within, glorious sparks
I do not recognize.

Chimes

Surely this
Knowledge of
The wing on which
These are the gates
That roll along
From unbroken
To the dead of
Sceptres sway

For thee

For thee

For thee

Grey

A return to my roots, my inner wolf. The lead around a radioactive sample. Woolen blanket by the fire. Anatomy of indecision. In the kitchen of industry, grey recovers the history of dust. Less flimsy than periwinkle, more functional than fun. Pervasive as yeast. My shoulder angel and devil blowing smoke. Uniform of conformity. Like doubled-die dimes, my flaw is my best feature.

Handbells

If the whole body were a hand…

Pavlov rings true:
Every part suffers.

Because I am not an eye.
Sparrows.

We, the beam, the shaft, the bolt.
A tower recumbent.

Parts that seem weaker.
The white rabbit will fall.

A body of symbols
clanging.

Where would the sense of smell be?

Parts that interpret:
I need you.

A red herring salivates.
Because I am not an ear.

My body of hands
shaking.

I made Jesus-shaped pancakes but I burned them. Am I going to hell?

Did the Jesuses run together?
The hems of their robes touch?

What were the signs it was time
to turn him over?

When you lifted him,
did his bodies break?
Did they leave their outline
on your non-stick pan?

What would Jesus do
if you left him gooey?
Do you wonder:
Perhaps he prefers
to be enflamed?

Did you tip the bottle
and pour out
every last drop
of maple syrup
at his feet?

Maroon

Old blood and long waits for rescue. The towel set I took to college, the itchy turtleneck I tore off as soon as I got home. Deeper than wine, with none of burgundy's formalities, all my first car's get-up-and-go, maroon steers clear of girlish drama. From the French for *chestnut*—fruit of hard luck and mastery—at one end: a flame. At the other: a scar. The first cultivated carrot. The light through closed eyes. My thoughts as they plunge.

If you die in Canada do you die in real life?

If you die in Canada, the bears beat their breasts
until the berries in their fists bleed, and the Mounties
ride backwards.

If you die in Canada, you fall through the ice
and land in Michigan.
At 7:30 in Newfoundland, the wood for your casket
will be harvested—sustainably—by David Suzuki
and the Beachcombers.

Die in Canada and the Canada geese
fly in a lowercase v.

If you die in Canada, you've lived
in Canada: the tilled,
the untold.

And if you die tonight, without me near,
dear brother—all of Canada
will be sorry.

Acoustic Guitar

Campfire honest, that boy—
winter wheat and bird's eye
sweetness. Dog-eared down-
beat, doorjamb. Tarnished clasp
slips, gingerly truffled
Kumbayotic elation. Midnight
trampoline: picked at sixteen, palm
along your neck, pin-
feathered. Lick, riff
—only takes
a spark.

Vermilion

Burning sulfur and heavy mercury. Dragon's blood. Like childhood, it darkened over time. Created shadows where Michelangelo wanted highlights—giving rise to the Apostle John's billowy breast. Presses the dot on a woman's brow—where creation begins.

On Earth as It Is

Marimba

If nymphs on enoki
        and snails with toes

If dwellers in glass houses
        if these stones stay silent

If ichor droplets
        the size of hamsters

If two birds in the sky
        see one in a hand

If the earth crumbles
        between your fingers

If life hands you lemurs
        or you smell truffles

If you could
        choose your own trance

Umber

Somber yew. Rust-stained horses gallop through ancestral slumbers. Tree bark hovering as moth. Flesh, a whiff of scorn, the vaguest of doubts. Mmm. brr.

Pan Flute

solfa

falsetto   larkspur

homespun *halleluiahs*

sfumato hours   wistful ghost haunts the toothless mists

  in the marsh   an egg cell divided

  cypsela   wafting snow

Would it be possible to shoot down the moon?

men have shot down men
for the sin of loving
other men

men have shot down women
for the sin of walking a dog
at dusk

children have shot down babies
students—teachers
fathers—sons

one night a hunter
raised his AR-15
pulled the trigger

and shot at the moon
after a poem
called it *tender*

its wounds may
be mistaken
for a face

Red

Audacious is just perfect for the everyday lip. My locker stuffed with roses *to* ... my name misspelled. Objects disappearing in space look redder. (Let's blast ableism on the next Falcon Heavy—watch it bleed.) The past tense of read—a future reaping. If this had been a real emergency, you would have heard my cry for help. Red dye makers begged glass artists to stain the devil blue. Prayers unanswered. A tomato touches down beside the scarecrow. Red walls make us move faster, find anyone more attractive. Ready? Crack a can of bull. This old thing? Roll out the carpet for the pretenders. Maybe someday I'll come out as atypical. My erogenous zone is under the poetry. I want to want to want you.

Tambourine

patchy chive
nitty-gritty

kitschy church
chorus charisma

wet dog
cheat checklists
achieve itchy

child child child child
child child child

chink in your armour
chink in your armour

clink of your
clink of your
clink of your
chagrin

Prussian Blue

The deepest blue—discovered by a desire for red gone wrong. Neighbour to darkness. Chemical reaction between iron bars and the smell of fear. Before we synthesized sadness, painters bartered for single drops bled from stone. Ingesting Prussian blue may save from radiation. Opa told me we came from Prussia, but our attempts to recreate the sky lacked permanence. My shadow—a blueness that cannot be bottled. Even rhesus monkeys choose blue. Over anything else. Don't touch me.

Have you ever kissed a raccoon?

Carry me to the peak
of a prairie elevator
while the carwash sleeps.

Curl up with me
in a bed of shredded
drywall and hay.

Take me into the trees
to nibble foraged raspberries,
pb on rye.

Turn me over and over
in your deft hands
under the clear lake.

The chimes inside me:
foremilk and wind.
For the love of God,

let rabies be a lie.
Press your nose to mine.
Remove your mask.

Harmonica

Rocking streetcar
Barstool heartrate
Scraggly conundrum
Scramble scree
Flam a shim
Brylcreem fulcrum
Comb in my pocket
Milkshake possum *mmmm*
Chuff more than you can chew
Fiddlehead and bugleweed
A burr is a seed
From the farm we came
To the farm we shall return

**Is it possible we are ghosts trying to find out
why we died and where we belong?**

Blow out a candle, my feet are cold.

The dog rests
her velvet head against them. Somewhere,

a yawning car responds to a roadside
bargain with the Divine.

This is what matters: ears

and the cats who wake without them,
the pyramids of hay

from which they
rise and stretch

their strings of light.

Fiddle

jetsam chilli dogs in Lilliput
intrepid day lilies
shimmy splendid daffodils

furtive ceilidh
didactyl
weedily soliloquize
peccadillo katydid

quayside quesadillas
antediluvian sidle
unbridle sordid cordillera

needle nibble nickel pickle
dribble diddle riddle

peach jam
thanks clam
chickaree

Yellow

Light at the end of the cave drawing. The mustard seed of faith can move molehills. Squeezed, it sings like a canary. The happy faces at Walmart. The *pip pip* of my baby's fistful of Cheerios. A caution tape barricade across my heart. *I can't believe you're not bitter!* Fifty metres beneath the sea, yellow wavelengths dissolve. In France, yellow cries *jealousy*; in Japan, *courage;* in Egypt, *mourning*. From the root *to shine*, yellow cracks the yoke I'm under. The pages where plastic surgeons come before plumbers. Did you notice I'm still holding a banana? If I make lemonade, someone will call me *brave*.

Where is the internet located? And is it open to the public? Would like to take my son to see it on vacation.

I took my son to Playland
and watched him tell every barefoot child
you require socks to play.
I took my son to school
and watched him prepare plastic eggs
on a cardboard stove.
I took my son to the edge of the lake
and snapped his photo before the cloud burst.
I took my son to the edge of what I knew
and we jumped in together.

Ukulele

A tickle, wrapped in a parody,
inside a chinchilla.
Flaps here is a flea.

Lament of the primeval,
by the peashooter,
for the free gull.

School me, balmy charm.
For sure, and Kevin hears a goat.

Do you remember the day you were born?

A sense of sprawl—
a poem you could fall asleep in.

There is no limit
to how short this poem can be.

The town itself shifts like sandpaper.
There is no end to childhood.

On the roof across from the café,
the red helicopter sets itself down.

You who were born
eating the world,

a poem is a sphere evolving.
Only the wind prevails.

Double Bass

In a nutshell
you're a cantaloupe

a hot air balloon
rising in a barrel

of moonlight
the grandfather clock

drips on the basalt
on every hour

gentle cannon
pointing to the stars

At what stage of their life do ants become bees?

In midlife. Sweeter, lighter. We cast off
the heavy crumbs we carried.

We no longer run. Unafraid to live high,
be left hanging. We do not hide.

We buzz. Not caring who is bothered.
We lose our bite and

hold tight our final sting.

Accordion

Lick cat   snort fumes   crinkle potato
Fan smoke   march paper doll chain
Pawn a sump pump hose   snorkel in suspenders
    Waffle with cilantro

The long and short of it is   the heart of cardboard
The warp and woo   wave akimbo
Grab a Hallmark lung   snoring oarsmen
    Grassy hillside calling

Green

Some days I mishear the most beautiful things. *Hit me with your vista—spidery waaaaave,* mondegreens: my muse. I'm on my knees. Sunlight says *go* to a pack of seeds and my potting soul. Charged with saving the earth. I dance in clover—the dress a million wouldn't buy me. My grass is always taller than the other side of the fence. Last one picked for baseball; now I'm closing the book. Normal is a setting on fire. Pay no attention to the voices behind the curtain, those wizards at ostracism. Each poem finds its own forest. *Would you, could you,* in this skin? Green is Ordinary Time: the path mortals walk between disturbance and glory. I am all the things I do not throw away.

If I eat myself would I become twice as big or disappear completely?

To taste the familiar and not be consumed by it.

To love myself as one loves a pizza.

To transform the world using only my mouth.

Like Alice in Wonderland, to shrink, to grow.

To fear no pain.

INDEX

Colours

Musical Instruments

Yahoo Questions

NOTES

The title of this book could also have been *Magen-TAAAH; For Mine are the Keys, the Hammers, the Flurry; Overdub Hubbub Bubaline Flub; Aqua Gong Pancakes; Magenta Brain Chimes.*

The epigraph is from Michael Moynahan, SJ. "Forgiving God?" *Hearts on Fire: Praying with Jesuits,* ed. Michael Harter, SJ. Chicago: Loyola Press, 1993. I discovered this prayer as I made the Ignatian Exercises from September 2022-May 2023 under the guidance of my spiritual director Mary Reimer. The Exercises were part of my two-year training in the Sustainable Faith School of Spiritual Direction under the instruction of Suhail Stephen and alongside my cohort: Ruth Braun, Deb Monk Small, Julia Stein Sandstrom, and Denver Wilson.

The section headings are excerpts from these Scriptures: "A bruised reed he will not break, and a dimly burning wick he will not quench" (Isaiah 42:3, NRSV). "Though I speak with the tongues of men and of angels, but have not love, I have become sounding brass" (1 Corinthians 13:1 NKJV). "Even before a word is on my tongue, O Lord, you know it completely" (Psalm 139:4 NRSV). "Then [Jesus] said to the man, 'Stretch out your hand.' He stretched it out, and it was restored, as sound as the other" (Matthew 12:13 NRSV). "May your will be done on earth as it is in heaven" (Matthew 6:10 NRSV).

The poem titles in the form of questions were all taken from anonymous inquiries found on Yahoo! Answers, a Q&A platform active from 2005-2021.

Musical instrument descriptions were facilitated by the *Vienna Symphonic Library* site www.vsl.co.at/en/Academy.

Colour poem research included the following websites: www.pantone.com; www.colormatters.com; www.arttherapyblog.com/online/color-meanings-symbolism; www.gemsociety.org; www.biotele.com; and www.visual-arts-cork.com/artist-paints/colour-pigments.htm; and books on colour history by Philip Ball, Joann and Arielle Eckstut, Victoria Finlay, Simon Jennings, Janice Lindsay, Matthew Dennison, Michel Pastoureau, and Stephen Quiller.

"Xylophone"—every letter in the alphabet begins at least one word because the instrument features in so many children's ABC books.

"Violet"—the line about longevity is based on Alexandria's Genesis, an online myth dating to 2005 that suggests a genetic mutation causes some individuals to become perfect beings with violet eyes and a lifespan of 150 years. www.medicalnewstoday.com

"Flute" hints at Ezra Pound's "Petals on a wet, black bough" from "In a Station of the Metro," in *Personae*, New Directions Publishing Corporation, 1926. The Latin for "receive," *Suscipe* is the name for a prayer of Ignatius of Loyola that ends, "Give me only your love and your grace, that is enough for me."

"Russet"—the reference to "fired clay" is in honour of my hero, friend, and pottery teacher Cliff Derksen October 27, 1945-May 22, 2022.

"Purple"—I learned that greenery was once purple from Ker Than's "Early Earth Was Purple, Study Suggests" in *Live Science*. Apr. 10, 2007. www.livescience.com/1398-early-earth-purple-study-suggests.html. "With a great big hug..." is from "I love you" by Lee Bernstein, popularized by Barney.

"How do you dress to look like a poet?"—the Elizabeth Bishop quote is from "One Art" in *The Complete Poems 1926-1979*. Farrar, Straus and Giroux, 1983.

"Do you think humans will ever walk on the sun?" was inspired by the painting "The Heavens Declare… The Skies Proclaim" by Angela Lillico.

"I was bitten by a turtle when I was a young lad, can I still drink orange juice?"—the stories are from www.theguardian.com: "Working USB stick found in leopard seal's year-old frozen faeces," Feb. 5, 2019; "Lego piece falls out of New Zealand boy's nose after being stuck for two years," Aug. 17, 2020; "Missing parrot turns up minus British accent and speaking Spanish," Oct. 17, 2014.

"Indigo"—I learned the folktale from reading Catherine McKinley's interview "Indigo: The Indelible Color That Ruled The World" on NPR, Nov. 7, 2011. See also her *Indigo: in search of the color that seduced the world.*

"How long can you keep a brain alive outside the body?" was written during my editing process with Jennifer Still, turning a manuscript of word and sound play into an exploration of joy on the other side of trauma. Since my first book about my children's autism spectrum disorder, I have also been diagnosed with ASD traits (partially explaining my sound and touch sensitivities), and I have begun processing the effects of missed attachment, childhood bullying, and religious trauma. The line "I'm on the inside, on which side are you" is from the children's gospel chorus "One Door," copyrighted by Coleman, 1933, found in *American Hymnal*, 477, composer unknown.

The cassette *Morning Like This* is by Sandi Patty (Word Records, 1986); the poem responds to the title song's lyrics: "Did the grass sing? Did the earth rejoice to feel You again? Over and over like a trumpet underground Did the earth seem to pound 'He is risen!'"

"How to get YouTube to come film you?" hints at Don McKay's "our heads full of closets,/our hearts full of ovens,/and our sad feet." from "Song for the Song of the Common Loon" in *Paradoxides*, McClelland & Stewart, 2012.

"Turquoise"—the William Wordsworth quote referenced is "Wisdom is oftimes nearer when we stoop than when we soar."

"Ecru"—toxic purity culture is the evangelical Christian emphasis on maintaining sexlessness of thought and deed until the wedding night—under threat of lifelong internal and external shame—with the promise of blissful marital sex to the obedient (assuming they can flip on the switch).

"Is the earth visible from earth? Just wondering…" was inspired by the painting "Heaven and Earth" by Genevie Henderson.

"What is heavier: a kilogram of steel or a kilogram of feathers?" is for Michelle Kauenhowen, Sept. 1, 1964- Nov. 8, 2018.

"Pink" references the anti-bullying "Pink Shirt Day," an annual event on the last Wednesday of February, which originated in Nova Scotia in 2007 when hundreds of students wore pink in solidarity with a classmate bullied for their pink shirt.

"Handbells"—italicized lines are from 1 Corinthians 12 (NIV).

"I made Jesus-shaped pancakes but I burned them. Am I going to hell?" hints at the woman healed by touching the hem of Jesus' robe in Matthew 9:20-22; Jesus' flaming anger at those cheating the poor in John 2:15; and Mary Magdalene's anointing of Jesus' feet with costly perfume in John 12:3.

"If you die in Canada do you die in real life?" is for Timothy Dale Falk, Dec. 1, 1979-Nov. 25, 2020.

"Marimba" contains a reversal of Luke 19:40: when religious leaders tell Jesus to rebuke the joyfully shouting crowd, " He answered, 'I tell you, if these were silent, the very stones would cry out'" (ESV).

"Umber" refers to the waved umber moth (Menophra Abruptaria) whose colouring looks like tree bark, making for nice camouflage.

"Prussian Blue" references the study "Spontaneous color presences in rhesus monkeys" in Behavioural

Processes, volume 174, May 2020, 104084, found on sciencedirect.com.

"Yellow" hints at the line "Did you notice I was holding a banana?" from my first book *Tell Them It Was Mozart* (Brick Books, 2016) about raising autistic children.

"Ukulele" is a misheard translation of these speeches: Winston Churchill's "a riddle wrapped in a mystery inside an enigma, but perhaps there is a key" (Oct. 1, 1939); Abraham Lincoln's Gettyburg Address: "government of the people, by the people, for the people" "Four score and seven years ago" (Nov. 19, 1863).

"Do you remember the day you were born?"— Phrases and ideas in lines 1–4 and 11 in the poem are from a conversation between Kaie Kallough and Deanna Young, hosted by McNally Robinson Booksellers and moderated by Charlene Diehl as part of Thin Air 2019 in Winnipeg.

ACKNOWLEDGEMENTS

The writer gratefully acknowledges the financial support of the Winnipeg Arts Council, Manitoba Arts Council, the Deep Bay Artists' Residency, the Canada Council for the Arts, and my parents during the creation of these poems.

Previous versions of several poems have appeared in the colour-swatch-style chapbook *Blue Moon, Red Herring* (JackPine Press, July 2019) and in the following periodicals: *Prairie Fire*, arcpoetry.ca, *Grain*, *Winnipeg Free Press*, *The Society 2018*, *Contemporary Verse 2*, *The New Quarterly*, *McMaster Journal of Theology and Ministry*, *Qwerty*, A) GLIMPSE) OF), *Understorey*, *NōD magazine*, and *Literary Review of Canada*.

A selection of musical instrument poems under the title *Bubaline Flubdub* was shortlisted (but not published) in the 2018 Frog Hollow Press chapbook contest. Under the title "Warming Up," a selection of brass poems ("Trumpet," "Trombone," "Horn," and "Tuba") placed second in *Prairie Fire's* 2016 Banff Centre Bliss Carman Poetry Award Contest. "Magenta" placed third in *Prairie Fire's* 2014 contest. A previous version of "Jet" was shortlisted for *Arc Poetry Magazine's* 2015 Poem of the Year. Gratitude goes out to all the above-mentioned publications' editorial teams and contest judges.

The author wishes to acknowledge these mentors, manuscript evaluators, and writers-in-residence for their feedback on portions of this collection: Joanne Epp, Alice Major, Lauren Carter, Gary Thomas Morse, Christine Fellows, John K. Samson, Steven Ross Smith, Jeanne Randolph, Madhur Anand, the JackPine Press board, Write Ramble, and the Electronic Garret.

Huge thanks to everyone from At Bay Press— especially Matt Joudrey for picking me for his author team. And a big box of cookies to my editor Jennifer Still for listening with me and encouraging me to put more of my heart on the line.

Thank you to my family, Tony, Kieran, and Gemma, and to my friends from Hope Centre Ministries, st benedict's table, and Imago Dei Christian Community for giving me a safe place to be weird.

AUTHOR

Angeline Schellenberg is the author of *Tell Them It Was Mozart*, winner of the Lansdowne Prize for Poetry and Eileen McTavish Sykes Award for Best First Book and finalist for the national Relit Award. Her second collection, *Fields of Light and Stone*, was shortlisted for the 2022 KOBZAR Book Award. Recipient of the 2017 John Hirsch Award for Most Promising Manitoba writer, Angeline has also published chapbooks with The Alfred Gustav Press, Kalamalka Press, Dancing Girl Press, and Jack Pine Press. She is a contemplative spiritual director, assistant photographer, writing mentor, and the host of Speaking Crow—Winnipeg's longest-running poetry open mic. Angeline lives on Treaty 1 Territory with her husband, their adult son and daughter, a rescue dog, and not nearly enough plants.

Photo – Anthony Schellenberg

OUR AT BAY PRESS ARTISTIC COMMUNITY:

Publisher – **Matt Joudrey**

Managing Editor – **Alana Brooker**

Substantive Editor – **Jennifer Still**

Copy Editor – **Courtney Bill**

Proof Editor – **Danni Deguire**

Graphic Designer – **Lucas c Pauls**

Layout – **Lucas c Pauls and Matt Joudrey**

Publicity and Marketing – **Sierra Peca**

Thanks for purchasing this book
and for supporting authors and artists.
As a token of gratitude, please scan the
QR code for exclusive content from this title.